ANGLES AND CIRCLES

Poems

Sad Grave of an Imperial Mongoose, 1973
Penguin Modern Poets 23 (with Edwin Muir and Adrian
Stokes), 1973
Discoveries of Bones and Stones, 1971
Ingestion of Ice Cream, 1969
A Skull in Salop, 1967

Anthologies

Faber Book of Love Poems, 1973
Faber Book of Popular Verse, 1971
Unrespectable Verse, 1971
Rainbows, Fleas and Flowers, 1971

Criticism and Celebration

The Contrary View, 1974
Notes from an Odd Country, 1970
Poems and Poets, 1969

ANGLES AND CIRCLES
AND OTHER POEMS

Geoffrey Grigson

LONDON
VICTOR GOLLANCZ LTD
1974

1.

821
GRI

*Printed in Great Britain by
The Camelot Press Ltd, Southampton*

For H. M. J. G.

You have not lost the key.
On the far side are
The Morning Glories
And the Belles de Nuit.

Acknowledgments
Poems in this collection have first appeared in the *Listener*,
Encounter, *Antaeus*, the *New Statesman*, the *Sunday Times*, the
Times Literary Supplement, *Poetry*, and the *London Magazine*.

Contents

Entente Cordiale
For the Common Market

O happy land where senators evade
The taxes by the vicious workers paid,
Where, like the courtyard gravel from the pits,
The newly born are graded and their futures fixed,
Where painted wells are built from worn-out tyres
And prefects are corrupted liars
Who boast and boast of scintillating glory
Invisible in the national story;
Where guiltless effluents foul each river
And brutal marc breaks down at last the liver,
Where rusting shacks defile the sand
All along the glittering Biscay land;
Where art can get no dole from trade
And meanness rules, so frescoes fade
And oak saints on their altars crumble
And medieval donjons likewise tumble—
Land of Algerian wines, and Catholic trance,
My three times happy, three times fertile France
Whose genial yes enamels Fascist no,
Whose stunted infants only fail to grow,
Many are the reasons why I love you so.

Tired from being, unfresh plants are dying,
A scent of matted nettles
Makes an atmosphere.

I recall, there was a battle here,
A thousand—that means many—sprawling, kites,
Crows, a scent of dying.

Blood and disembowelling in the still dry
Autumn of campaigning. Defeat, fear, being caught
In the early dying

Light, or if escape,
Complaining, not any
Hopes at all remaining.

Two A.M.

Distant, clear, down low,
Are lights of men,
From on top of the great lateral hills.
The automatic revolving lighthouse of the oceanic
Island throws—and beyond doubts of
Warning and of safety—a far
Question, question into emptiness.

And all emptiness, all gravity,
Ultimacy, nothingness, are then
By us felt and seen. And we
Are small, instant, here.
And time is all round and all
Elsewhere; of which one other island now strikes
Two a.m. in the night somewhere.

Two hours more, then over
Sierras, monadnocks, lakes, prairies, taiga, ice,
Cays whitened by noddies, seas and seas and soiled
Tarred shingles, lightens a huge sky-
Arch, geranium-red, partly, so that we,
Spiders, blue neon flies, gay birds
Etcetera, etcetera, in sun, are small, instant, here.

At least now, with our bodies close,
Be comforted.

Young and Old

You are young, you two, in loving:
Why should you wonder what endearments
Old whisper still to old in bed,
Or what the one left will say and say,
Aloud, when nobody overhears, to the one
Who irremediably is dead?

Monsieur Colin's Paint-box Garden

This July are few famous flowers
In Monsieur Colin's garden,
He died in the cold and rain.

And Madame Colin will not go into
Monsieur Colin's garden.
The green weeds are there again.

The first for fifty years
In Monsieur Colin's garden,
And they need little rain.

Dry flowers are choked by them
In Monsieur Colin's garden,
Savages camped there again.

Madame Colin will not look back
At Monsieur Colin's garden
When she leaves finally in November's rain.

And next will go up tall swings
In Monsieur Colin's garden,
Children running, savages turned out again.

Trôo

To Wystan Auden

They said, Have you heard the news?
Serious they looked, were grey, and I guessed
Someone they and I held in affection
Was dead. Then they said, Auden is dead,
Then they said it was you.
They had caught a flash of your death
On the air. Out of doors was it cold
Ending of English September, soon
To be frozen. Tobacco flowers lagged and sweet
Peas waved on their shoulder. You were dead.
Later I waited. I heard an announcer say
We must catch up with the weekend news, and there
Sure were you, there flashed on your big
    Wrinkled phiz. But O
It was still, still as now must you
Always be seen. You were held there a second,
And O you had died in a second, without
Being ill as you feared.

Forty years now
Have slipped by since for some who were young
You became living's healer, loving's
Magician, for all of these years
The imposer of blessings.
You were our fixture, our rhythm,
Speaker, bestower, of love for us all
And forgiving, not of condemning, extending
To all who would read or would hear
Your endowment of words. There was a time—
I recall—when you were not. Once more
You are not. But time, after you, by you
Is different by your defiance.
In Vienna dead on a day
When the displaced by violence out

16

On the airport were practising violence,
When at home a mad politician prophesied
Violence, enjoying dismay. But this morning
Is different, my dear one. As well as
Your words are you here who will address
Us and bless us more, and no more.
In death you are living, and this
Is not the end of a day.

An Autumnal

Because gunmen kill hostages in banks,
Because gunmen are gunmen and
Because police torturers are police torturers
On account of their genes and their mothers,
Because there are massacres,
Am I not to say that I love you?

Who is helped if I refuse to say
There now are yellow leaves, sky-blue
Morning Glories and this
Morning-Glory-blue sky above you,
Or if I decline to admit
That tendernesses glove you?

With Loving and with Women

To be obsessed with loving and with women—
Well, why not? It is obsession with
Impossible completion, and with benediction.
Da nobis pacem—but with that peace, as well
Exhilaration.

Under Alkanet

Not quite still or too fierce that sharp
Cypress air, and not more than lightly
Or slightly thinking, either one of us then, of
What had nested certainly there,

You lay in the shadowed stone coffin;
Under blue alkanet, your bright
Head in the socket, between breasts your two palms,
Parodied death and prayer.

Steps crushed the gravel. Quickly upright,
And confused, you dusted dead
Leaves from your skirt, and shook
Death from your hair.

Big clouds shouldering
Over hills of green or black
If near;
Such clouds shouldering
Over hills blue if
Not near and on the high
Side of this island
Should stay longer,
And not have to rise clear
Off such various hills,
Not then have to loosen.
Not to have to thin, and
Not to have to disappear,
"Spiritually" (which
Isn't what I would say
But I see why they
Said it) into the greater
As it seems blue air.

This Year the Dove

A sub July. Inside our hedge this year
Does the chilled
Dove not play
Incessantly her throat.

I see not one unconcerned dove
On the road; which then lifts, with no
Alarm, to a wire. Days heavily
If damply heated these presences

Prefer; in such from a depth coolly
Do they send their
Monotonous
Unmonotonous note

In the Crypt at Bourges, the Effigy
of Jean Duc de Berry

You rest, your neat slippers rest
On your fast asleep bear in this
Crypt down here where they tomb every
Straw-seated grey broken chair.

Risbec, Meurice, hundreds more
Have incised their names up
And down in the soft grey
Polished stone of your gown.

Your eyes too are closed like
Your bear's, your mouth at last
Is turned down, the tip of
Your snub nose has gone.

Grey. Down here, alabaster duke, is
Not one gay coloured item of day,
Grey have become your tender rich
Hours, without flowers.

Metre of Recent Living

In our metre

Bells are rung,
Our river fills with Tide,
Our middle of the morning
Train rolls down,
Little foxes
Cross the ride
Where their great-great-
Grandmas died.
Choirboys frilled
Like peach-fed hams.
Dirty-minded little rams,
Every weekend
Trill to Heaven,
And in his flat
Magnificat
Our Left Foot
Sings to grander
Bevan.
On the *Times*
Now summer's come,
We flea the cat
Upon the page which
Features Levin.
Aimless cabbage-
Whites arrive,
The founder's silly
Lecture's given.
Marked by earrings
Thighs declare
Lady poets too
Are queer.
Impudic fungi

Smell like sin.
Seville oranges are in.
Various Pakenhams
Thick as rooks
Now bring out
Their autumn books,
And stand, but not
Like Ruth forlorn,
Among the stubbles
Of the porn.
Black rolls the smoke
From dawn to dawn.

    So this year
    Our measure goes
    Not quite as sweetly
    As a rose
    Yet not exactly
    Flat as prose.

Visit, and Variation
Without Guilt

When I lean my head back on my hands
And Vega is up there still above my nose
And hoarse young owls who have not learned
Their flutes are calling, and I expect
Another Leonid to be falling,

Candles light these talkers up, who break
Their peaches into two. He's cotton close on top,
She's coiled red hair, her Turkish
Earrings sway, she's aged; she is tired, having
Driven from the boat all day.

I think I hear her say
"Don't you agree?" Without words I say
"We're on the Earth, the two of you
And me," and thanks, without guilt, for this cooled
Earth, and them, flow out of me.

I don't notice what they say, they are
Friends, who have made a long detour. Before
Heat to-morrow creates another
Shrivelling midday deeper into decline of life
They will have driven away.

Autumnal

"Spectacles on my nose and autumn in my heart"—I. Babel

I suppose it wouldn't do—I mean it—to express that way
what used to be expressed by saying that the
leaves are falling.

Leaves aren't in every cognizance but all the same it's
really true that everywhere at least inside
the Northern Hemisphere the
leaves are falling.

There is a story of two maiden sisters in an upper flat
who could think only of a drift of leaves inside a
London (East End) park for
burying their cat.

They weren't much cognizant of leaves, but having had that
business with their cat, I think they'd take my meaning,
now I mention that once more the
leaves are falling.

And there's a critic for whom the interesting life
in literature is always black; for him leaves were not,
are not, never will be leaves at least on
trees, so never, never
can be falling.

But—though they're appalling—I cannot bother with
that rotten critic or that putrefying cat: with no
finality, without a supercilious that's that, I only mention
to myself—it's true, it's autumn almost, and
it's nothing new—all day, all day the altered
leaves are falling.

W.'s Daffodils

I was going up a wide lane, of stems,
You were ahead and you would not turn
When I saw and called about—you
Had passed them, seen them already—

His celebrated wild single, among slight
Leaves of course twittering daffodils,
Though spring was over. Then until
I woke entirely I unclearly cogitated

His hard farmer-seeming head, how
At least the chin and the mouth of him
Inclined to laughter, sweetly, no
Matter what came after. Then between

Sleeping and being as I say awake
Entirely, getting this down, I worried:
To stop, enjoy, pick up, to mend
What I do declare I love;

To stop, sometimes; you indifferently
Ahead—it was a lane, and not a lake,
Lanes do go on and bend. So on, on until—
In this bed? Softly? Insensibly?—an end.

Red on Blue

In her red night dress she leans
Into a blue space of night
A black-blue space of night:
She looks into this night: her elbows

Touch the sill, I see, I draw
Her so before she turns. In red
Her upper arms and forward
Shoulders are

Against this blue of night.
Which blue night she does not see,
Which blue night's air she does
Not feel. I draw her so,

And she draws back and turns.
Slightly she smiles.
Through the wide openness,
The empty space of blue.

Another June

Let's think of June, which corresponds
To twenty-eight in women.

Petals of clumped peonies, it's true,
Have started falling.

But holidaying ants, and humans, so far
Are not swarming,

Winds are not driving, clouds are not
Blackly storming.

Even nights, as well as days, at last
Are positively warming.

To mutter "June is bluff" must be
Considered boring.

Were you asleep to all this summer stuff,
You would be snoring.

What we suppose repetitive may
Set us yawning.

But what else than Now is deity,
And worth adoring?

Note for Examiners

Late were Yeats and Tennyson
Virgins. Then as if all his years
Were lost and only nature left,
Into old age silver Tennyson
Wrote splendidly of sadness,
But ripe Yeats wrote in fury
Of defiant madness.

L'Ile Verte

(Site Classée. Camping Interdite)

Describe this celebrated site to me. Well,
First it is the clouds I see as rosy as small roses
Which are enclosing now a paring of a moon.
I see the yellowing *vert* of very slender trees

Aspiring past these rosy clouds to blue
(Of course, this setting shining paring
Of a moon is new). The clucking
Mobilettes have crossed, at last, the chattering

Bridge of wood, and they have vanished
Cheerfully through the lea, leaving this
River scene, tender like the young on mobilettes,
To all the scattered paper and to me.

Light noises from slight birds
In trees which have not leaves,
And through white sunshine waftings
Of now warmer, warmer air. Each

Season I arrive it seems that dying
Momentarily recedes. The mercury
Stays up. I'm told, I soon forget, who
Went earlier in the coldness of the year.

This time—the mercury pushes higher—
It was, for one, Bertin *menuisier*:
In hospital one week he had no visit
From his wife. And he remembered in his bed

His young first wife, whose death
of T.B., at eighteen, he said,
Had cheated him of life (a baggy, dirty,
Tough grub was his second wife).

Now they would have cured her of T.B.,
Large Bertin said and said;
Who knew, O yes, that he was dying.
Of oak so many times he had made

A happy bed: in his iron dying
Bed—the mercury goes higher—only about
This loved first girl was large dull Bertin
Talkative, and silent, and then sighing.

A Matter of James
(and Conrad)

I read of this man with despair.
I despair that after all I live elsewhere.
"Artist to artist talks": all I can do
Is read of this man with despair.

He read the other (he said so) like music rare,
Equal to equal, yet the circle with the square,
Surrendering to him to the deepest depth
He knew the good of him he could but fear.

"Art makes life": the artist's life is only there.
Deep was his life, restrained, austere;
Art being the harshest life to live of all
I read of this man with despair.

Unposted Reply

Of bright energy renewed slowly every
Bright morning less we retain. No more
Enough to make illumination fully
Again and again below unpromising rain.

Yet you have been, your letter says,
With your Especial Friend, in
Wharfedale in the rain laughing,
In a sports car, drawing bridges,

Seeing grey with mauve and with deep
Green a brown, object
Of you and Wharfedale and of rain.
Never, unless I prod you,

Do you say that you are old.
And I lament, and I should write
Content instead of this a shape
Like one you draw, or such

A plateau as you carve,
An Object, green with brown,
Which may be carried and unpacked, exhibiting
Your joy, in Rome, or Bonn.

The Bell

It was hair-raising,
A bereft woman's single
Moan, which I suddenly
Heard rising from down deep
Nearly to a yell

Behind elms greening. Birds
Called, lilacs were scent, coupled
Two black and scarlet
Beetles across sand. And I
Waited for the bell.

The Touches of Loving

I love affection
When I see a hand, in
Conversation,
Touching, in love,
Another hand, my
Feeling is
Exhilaration.

Or when I see
Touched by a hand,
Fluffed out, a cat,
Conforming quietly
To the warming
Contours of a lap, I love
Affection.

And after I see these
Touches of affection between
Two I seldom see
Or two unknown to me,
I am caught for a long while
By a scent
Of recollection.

One Surface of Loving

How is it I have not celebrated
Your under-arm, from your wrist
To your elbow?

It is one of your
Gentlest surfaces, and at this moment
It lies on my cheek.

I have only to turn my head
Very slightly and my lips are
Against this surface of loving,

But you remove your arm from me
And instead you are now
Stroking my head.

Have I the "Spirit of Orthodoxy"?
I have not. But have I
The spirit of opposing? Perhaps—

I remember my mother complaining
"Criticize when you have a home
Of your own, if you ever have one."

And I "believe in Utopia"?
No. But it is a proper idea,
Utopia. It is proper to hope.

That "things may be better", for instance,
And go on being better. It is proper
Not to piss our corrosion over

The beds of the flowers. If miracles will
Not occur, there should be
Mutations; not that I fancy

Either Christ with a pistol (he used,
I reflect, to turn us over,
Naked, to demons) or Big Shots

Whose nature and actions are mercy.
For my neck not the stiff collar
Of the Men of State, or of God,

And not that soft collar God's Men
Affect when they ape us
In a bonhomous mufti,

And not the kind worn open in sleet
By free-thinking offspring of Shelley,
Aggressive, and Left untenderly.

No medals, no citations, no codes
Of conclusions, by which all notions
Are infamous or accepted.

I do not decline that cress
May be pure and green on
Water running over red quartz,

That fine sand may be printed
Delicately by birds of the tide
Fringes, there a minute ago.

Light I ask for, not with excess
Of cold or heat, strong sufficiently
To reveal, to you and to me:

Element, congratulating,
Accentuating, of a perfection
Which we can think of only;

Or not think of, fatally—
Cold, tentative, in the fog
Wavering, and finding only

The semen of evil, the source
Of rejection, feeling of less,
Obsessive mildew of

Being always indifferent. In light
With light shall we enshrine the word
Enough till it sparkles, meaning

Enough now of plenty, but far from enough
Of extending and of dividing.
Inside red Ayers Rock

Rock crystal signed what inside
Our acts and our bodies
We are. It was light stronger

For darkness around, and made pure
From parching excess of heat
In the open. I say

Light is a centre correcting
Angles to nimbi, and in them,
In them we live.

Interview

May I ask you some questions, Mr. Dromgoole?
Are you (poetically speaking of course)
Of the very lower middle class?
Are your teeth (metaphor of verse) bad?
Were you (speaking again poetically-metaphorically)
Paunchy at twenty, bald at thirty,
And at fifty now
Are you deficient, defeatist, sad?
Do you elevate these—well, must I say
Characteristics and feelings
Into universals, Mr. Dromgoole?
Must we all—I mean is it the duty
Of us all to feel
Deficient, defeatist and sad?

Oh, Mr. Dromgoole,
Must we belong to your school,
Whose Hippocrene is a rill
Through the drab mud of an estuary
Of industry up in the north?
Would you decline to paddle, even if invited,
(I believe you would), Mr. Dromgoole,
With the wild swans of Coole,

Mud in your toes, Mr. Dromgoole,
Mud in your toes.
Button up, just blow your nose,
Just comb your hair, button
Your flies, just tell me,
Mister or D.Phil. Dromgoole.
Stop acting the fool.

Papposilenus

I knew, deceased, an Irish baronet and writer
Who drove a punt hard through reeds to land,
Picked up the slight girl (yes he'd picked her up)
Who was his passenger, and said I am going to be
A satyr now, and gallop with you through the trees.
Balls, cried she, and wriggled free, and hacked
Him there. She did not know what satyrs actually were,
Having no Latin and no Greek, but adequate
Lower education, so to speak.

Consequence of a Full Bladder

Kir, coffee, calva, so I woke
And dawn, as I. Babel wrote, then "drew
A streak along the far end of the earth".

I slept and woke: now rounded an elegant
Thunder-rose, a Zephyrine Drouin over this
End of the earth up high, up high.

I was awake for rain: bats at my end
Of the earth had wrinkled into cracks, swifts
Of August flew down low,

Down low some pink mist held
Our plain, thunder, silence, drops,
Drops on butt lids, then

Butting butting butting of the suddenly
Excessive absolute rain, and I exclaim how it
Darkened our, and I. Babel's, earth deeply again.

Trôo 1973

Items of a Night

Of the moon only a dull
Speck of orange I see now.
And in the course of these
Twelve words occurring
This speck of moon has gone
And a meteorite has
Straight downwards fallen.

I was with you two,
Below our gate we counted
Constellations. The moon
Was interfering. You're
Indoors, now. I lagged,
The moon's diminished, gone,
One meteorite, I say,

Has vertically fallen.
I turn. Car lights from under
Are patterning a play
Over our midnight cliffs.
Your lights are out. I think
Under these gleams and cliffs
By now you both are sleeping.

Sunshine will have you up
By eight to-morrow.
There will be dry wind
And heat. By midday will great
Melon leaves be drooping.
News will have come, this peace
May then be broken.

Or am I lying? Shall
I wake up before the morning

Much as I walk to bed, and both
Of you, uncertain, who am
Always to the low tide
And bared rocks of un-
Peacefulness so easily awoken?

The First Folio

I have, sir, the First Folio
Of your works, in facsimile at last
In a case, wrapped up in a parcel.

Which though a fortnight has elapsed
I have not opened yet. It is a very fine
March morning. I shall cut the tape, remove

Your works from their case
And open them I think to-day. But hesitate.
What shall I read first?

Shall it be your sunburnt sicklemen?
Your brightest angel that fell? Your
Sea of this world chafed on

The Kentish pibles? I am not young,
But certain events always
Are present: Shall it be therefore

On such a night as this? Or may my choice
Happen to be in a Quarto only? Your wand
Broken, you would advise me

Cynically to risk making a *sors Shakespeari-
ana* in your Shut Book? That, sir,
I resolutely do refuse.

Stormy Effects

Rain. We stood by a ford,
Were unsure under the hull of a storm
Which sheered up, which was lit
By wide sun, and then stiffer and stiffer

Drove the rain down. And we had to run
Uphill to her home by the track
Which had been a heated hard
Brown before. Now wet to herself,

To her skin, she stood in her door
And she saw that I saw through her
Sodden white shirt
To the forms of her shoulders and breasts

Of which her loose shirt had given
No more than a hint before. She laughed,
She stared at the rain, I
Stared at her in the door.

The Great Bridge

Eyes are raised to the great bridge only,
And when this great bridge came
The ancient village here was done for.
Speedily did the great bridge thieve its name.

Nobody now wonders at the chalk cliffs,
Sees the church or yellow castle on the bluff.
Eyes lift from long barges creeping under;
Barges, wide river, and the high bridge are enough.

Heroes of guidebooks lived here, heroine
Of the castle was that sad Scotch queen.
They are forgotten here, the great bridge
Being absolute hero of the scene.

It darkens: a grand bow of lessening
Studs of light hangs on the high air.
A barge of new cars moves under. Cars, cables,
Piers, swim of reflections, gently disappear.

Hypnotized by this abstraction high in air,
Whistler, Hiroshige, are the words some say.
For the lighted bow articulates: it is not Then,
But Now; which is the better way.

Le Bernica

(*from the French of Leconte de Lisle*)

Lost on the mountain side, between two high walls
Of rock, it is a savage nook of dream that few
Have visited since years began,
Too high for sounds of ocean on the coasts
Below, or—forget them here—the sounds of man.

Sated with honey, curled hornets sleep
Inside delicious bells which creepers
Hang in the still air.
A curtain of aloes guards access, and springs
From fissured rocks tinkle and echo here.

Dawn throws a rosy bandeau round the height
Above this closed paradise of scented green,
And round the peaks there rise and run
Fresh tourbillons of violet mist, when this deep
Incense-burner meets the sun.

And when white lava of cloudless noon pours
Down, it sends small flashes only through
The denseness of the trees, which pass
Like liquid diamonds from branch to branch, sowing
Specks of fire upon a night of grass.

Sometimes, ears pricked, eyes sharp, and neck
Up straight, and dew along its flanks,
A kid jumps nimbly from the trees,
And drinks, its four feet set upon a shaking stone,
From hollows crowded with green leaves.

Birds swarm round, birds flit, from tree to moss
Upon the rocks, from grass to flower.
Some wet their emerald breasts,
Some dry their plumage in the heated breeze, preen
With thin beaks, and whistle by their nests.

They sing and sing, in chorus suddenly, mix
Warbling with their calls of joy, along with laughing
Notes their love-complaining goes.
But still these harmonies with such gentleness float
That the untroubled air continues in repose.

Only my spirit penetrates, breaks into this delight,
Plunges into the happy beauty of this world, feels
Itself running water, light, flower, and bird.
It assumes your dress, O primal purity, and
Rests in deity without a word.

This Nameless Place

As if—as if in a nameless
Corner to which come
Few, where grass is
Turf by nature,

Projecting rock
Serene, running water
Clear, where stems of the perfect
Trees are clean.

Not with you even
Can I go back to this
Nameless place
In my half-dream.

Gale in the Nesting Time,
by an Avon Bridge

Being a bird, having so to navigate
This fisty gale in its
Third morning would no doubt be weakening,
If one was an old bird.

It would not surely be
Exhilarating for a young bird; now
Being when especially birds take
Lowest, most straight courses.

Secretively they go, glide,
To nests. Of weathers
For them worst are these Shakespearian
Winds of May and leaping

Willows, as in that eighteenth
Sonnet, I would say, pushing
The car, pattering
Vegetation on the bonnet.

Grace Acts of Ourselves

Of grace acts of ourselves, of e.g. temples if in
Ruins on red rock, and gods (the better ones)
If with good sense now deposed, carvings
In cliffs of Buddha, books of hours, cities (few
Of them); of states of mind; fictions—all fictions,
Yes—in which is
What we name our spirit;—of these grace acts
And not excluding graces of the natural which also
Are, and which suggest; having of all these
Consolatory things so little sensed, is it—
Come clean on this, my few, few friends
Consoling that on dying soon our
Livingness depends?

After the Party

They have gone—empty our rooms are
Except of you and me; and we walk
Out, into the slight rain.

Yes, cut and level is the relentless
Grass, we imagine trees performing
A laying on of hands, we observe

Late spreading of the great catalpa's leaves,
Agree to parade a garden is sweet, arms around
Each other, after they have gone.

Three Bedroom Verses

i

The room I wake in, I am glad to say,
Has a window facing east.
There the sun surmounts
A bar of hill. This fact elevates
And tames the beast.

ii

How is it on some shiny mornings that
Disparate poems come in pairs?
I can't dress, I have chilled feet,
I have to write again,
I have not invited words.

iii

In living it is a peculiar day
When catching his body in his
Young wife's long
Mirror, a husband
Sees
His bush is grey.

After a Dream

God knows how often I dream of you,
After these years and years.
Then again we are in harmony,
I am again on the edge of your mystery,
You again on the edge of me. Awake, then
I know how I need you, but then, O then
I know that I made you.
Fifty miles away from me,
It would be useless to see you.

That Fat Rose

I chucked that fat rose, it seemed scentless,
That I did not know the name of,
Next to me, on the black seat of the car.
Then drove away. I saw big drops
Spill from its close folds to
The black stuff of the car, and that
Surprised me. I did not realize
It had been picked after the heavy
Thunder shower. Before I was home
That cherry rose had dried, and I
Was surprised again, the scent of that
Fat rose now filled the car.
But given late that rose wasn't
Rose, it was by then no more
Than a flower, it was an object
Which I repeat had wetted the plastic
Black seat of the car.

Dreams of old men are their norm of being,
They stride, all of the day is theirs,
The colour of their flowers is brilliant,
And they dream of women.

Great Barge on Our Lake
Below the Mountain

Morning light over our lake comes to the mountain.
It sharpens, O how it renders more splendid,
Gildings, carvings, down low, all the way
Back to the stern of the great ceremonial

Boat, O how more brilliant, I am amazed, it renders
The long red of its slightly billowing awnings. A few
Striped figures continue to move round the decks,
They clean up, they throw things over the sides.

A few float off, over water of gold
And blue of the dawning, to sleeping.
All night, all night there has been music, of
Strings, controlled by the court musician. Fanfares

Intermittent have been followed by thrilling
Very clear echoes out of the mountain,
There have been toasts, wine poured on to snow,
Observation of ceremonies. There has been

All the night self-satisfaction, by torches all night
Reflections flickered in mirrors. All night plain
Women forgot they were plain, and all but a few
Men forgot those selves which they carried.

Having fixed a dry stone for my backside
I relax on this slope, again I regard
The dale: how, far away, twenty-four
Arches cross it, from shadow to shadow,
How without sound a train of linked
Beetles traverses, and makes off
For Scotland. I delay, don't scramble
Down to what I have come for. Below me,
The tips of Scotch pines; rooted, still
Lower down, in the secret garden. If
I go down, though I find no orchids, no umbels
Of purple small primroses (since
It's October), two streams will join,
Enclosing a vee-shape of green. One stream
Will flow out of darkness under a bluntness
Of sloping rock, one will ease out through
Bits of a cave roof which dropped and broke
Aeons ago; will gather, widen, curve
With minimal falls, to the joining.
Midges will rise. The grey winter bed
Of scooped rock above will be clean.
For colour, a farmer's blue plastic
Sack from floods of the winter
Will be wedged into rocks. A globule
Will shine in a cupped leaf of grey-green
Lady's Mantle. The great mountain, too,
Will appear over trees, half clouded
Or for a moment free; both thrusting
And resting, and always, if I look
That way, surprising. And I am sure
That by all of this hidden garden, under
The dull floor of this dale, which I am
Seeing again, I shall be coolly unmoved,
Though I shall wish to be moved.

Do I con myself if I explain that I did not
Come into it first with you,
When you were as well new found?
Blue it is overhead
As such a discarded blue sack, through air
Which is lucid and warm and should be
The agent of wonder. For me, this is late,
In a late month too; though I am not,
In the classic way, dejected.

Yesterday, first seen, you showed me
—Beyond Kirkby Lonsdale churchyard, along
The quiet of the Lune—Ruskin's View.
Conned, or no, late or no, I say
That was different. That was part of the hidden
Garden of you, which you allow me at times
To enter; miserable and cold as you had been
In the sarcastic school of old lezzes
—You pointed it out to me—high
Over the flats of the Lune, under the fell.

Scent Inclusive

Shit and lilies they say are scented
by different strengths of the same chemicals combined
i.e. that which is dropped on drives by curvings dogs and
that which scents obstinately gardens

In June, and funerals, and appealed much
to epicene painters in velvet jackets of the Ideal
concerned with the Virgin's white virginity or the sexless
insemination of white virtue.

Shit being shit still and Madonna lilies still
being flowers which break along green lines it does
to me appear that some noses need much rubbing in this
only apparent contradiction

Or in this varying volatility of an
identical substance there being shit in some
sweetness if not sweetness concealed at times in
some shits, in our accidental existence.

Call to a Colonel

Having just seen a clock
Which told our time in jerks
Outside an undertaker's shop
I rang a colonel up.

He said "I don't know who
The hell you are. I tell
You, no, I do not die.
I graff myself in lives that make

More lives. I am part
Of their permanent legacy. Goodbye."
That was his reply, colonels
Having selves easy to satisfy.

Rock, Sea Water, Fire, Air

Rock

Essential is rock: in its extrusions let it not be
Too soft and friable, so too slatternly. Also
Let it not be chalk. With that I am not at home.
Let it not be—as a rule—too hard, too rough,
Too resistant of hard frost. Granite (though not
Basalt) I refuse. For preference let it release
Water, admit roots, breed flowers.

Sea Water

The property of sea water is colour,
Let its blue become rather more blue
Than light blue. Then let it spread
Shallowly over light and extensive sand
Into selected bays,
Making it green, but with blue still as neighbour.

I speak of sea water
As not too cold anklet-water, not too cold
Thigh-water as well.
I speak of it also as that
On which reflections rarely may undistorted float
Before darkness puts colour out.

Fire

Is less common.
Muscles of bumble-bees generate heat on
Chilly days: fire is much
Enclosed. Fires I have made best
Aren't metaphors: they burn
Rubbish of gardens or of hedges
Till wet leaves
Explode, and released fed flames
Ripple up at last.

Air

Filling legged or breasted or big belly clothes
On lines on Monday—that is one thing.
But air does not have to move horizontally, does not have
To go violent, have to turn into power.
Air may rise also vertically
Supporting—along escarpments—gliders, birds
On infinite freshness, on which they play.
Especially good, not
Heated, not carrying frost, such air is at the
Beginning of a special day.

View of a Warped Coffin
on an Island seldom Visited

A coffin tight between tough jags of lava.
How was that? Had it a tenant?—other
Than red dust of lava fallen from always
Rising, running trades? Had it been a cradle,

Had it been a blue flecked
Easel on this ocean island left by Mr.
Hodges, artist, on the lava. A coffin,
Though, containing dust of lava?

People Divided, in a
Spring Month

White oil drums for a barrier;
To close what gap
There is does a car's extraordinary
Carcase stand on end.

A sentry in surly green
Comes out shabbily,
Examines, lets through one who's not
Detestable, if not a friend.

Houses. Are walls, no roofs,
No doors, no windows. And no
Hens. And what blue on to low
Rock creams, beyond. And round

Confabulate grayly most
Old olive trees. And what star-flowering
Weeds possess this now not turned
Hard orange ground.

The Landscape Gardeners

Brutal shuddering machines, yellow, bite into given earth.
Only rich Whigs, commanding labour,
Once had earth shifted, making lakes, and said
—And it was true—"We are improving Nature."

Somewhere

Our picnic ought to be in the morning,
When the sun rises,
When there is dew on our picnic table,
When the shadows of me, and you,
And of our picnic table, stretch far
(Into what could be the glade of an Elsheimer
    fable)
And I draw your two breasts (if I am not
More coarse) on the wet of the car,
And the sun rises and it lights
The half-rhymes, and there is
No one about,
And there is more
And more new light, not hard yet,
Nothing left of a night.

Take out the dry chairs, drink our coffee.
There are no fears.

Dulled Son of Man

Dark son of man, his hunched shoulders lifting,
Through tinted fog of frost goes down to work.
Green is reduced, of trees, distance
Accepting him is vague, grass of pleasure each
Side is frizzled gray. I know him. Grit is to be
Spread, ditches will be cleared, kerbs laid.

No, he is not wise. He does not envy scattering
Birds or, particularly, those that fly
Into this swallowing fog in white and scarlet
Cars. Man—his parent—ploughed up farms
And bent himself. Roads, roads, near Exit 22,
Are son of man's concerns. More cars

Swim by. Wrapped is son of man in his black
Torn coat (with yellowed shoulders, that he may be seen)
And Work, Work (the observing Philosophers do not
Observe) has screwed him too and gigantized his now
Warmed, hidden, hardened beetroot hands; which must,
Dull, dulled son of man, be taken out, and hold, and pull.

The One-eyed Archangel
in the Zoo

He dozes, pushed up against
The heavenward grille,
He comes to, he complains again
Of being ill,

Stretches, exhibiting his
Featherless middle,
Loosing now and then an arc
Of splendid piddle

On to the kids below, who laugh.
Then again he mopes,
And will not swing at all
Upon his shiny ropes.

He realized the muscles of his wings
Were getting flabby:
Couldn't he be tethered, for a change,
Inside the Abbey?

He would rise up to
The fan-vaulting there
And play to visitors, at stated
Times, the Trumpet Tune and Ayre.

He begged, Give me
A trump of gold.
The Commissioners refused, and said
The music rights were sold.

No jess would hold. In the Zoo, then,
Watch him raise a dry

Scaled lid and flash the diamond
Of his one remaining eye.

How his cage stinks! He'd dropped to Earth
To act the Heavenly Reaper,
Was caught, and how ashamed he is that
Man should be his keeper.

Television Tonight

A black fly is crawling. And as well across my screen
Are leaves—antique sense, antique
Word—falling. A girl

Walks up from the infinite point of perspective,
Closer; passes in the unending alley
What may be named the point

Of Most: of most emotion, most rejection, and
Most recollection; continues; leaves
Continue falling, the black

Fly continues diagonally crawling. Oh,
Abstractions, Figures, Closing, Soaring, Short-
Coming, Falling, Being Void, Being

Not Here—Abstractions, O as in my father's
Litany in the damp church have mercy, being
Us, and to us our whole time calling.

Tendernesses of those dead now
Do we not meet
Along our cold Albion Street.

As well as in poems, paintings, or
Quadrangles they contrived,
I say in a cloud,

In some slope or a coombe,
In pillows of cress, so green,
With white flowers, on a ford,

In a fawn beach seen, I declare,
May their tendernesses survive,
Encountering us, who are alive.

Encounter with a Kentish Bird

This parrot travels in a car,
He likes the way its engine purrs.
And tight his feathers fit. Best
Seen are tail feathers of the acid green

Of February nettles, light-
Edged each one with yellow. But
Some under-feathers of his wings
Are blue. About his cage, his home,

It would be foolish to suppose he should
Be flying past huge fluttering
Butterflies across the vaulting
Of a solemn jungle. This

Bird of Amazonian descent hatched
Out four years ago upon an avicultural
Farm in Kent. English as
Me or you, like most of us inside

The identical cage of "socio-
Economic forces" he's more
Or less, I fear, content. Certainly
Like me he does not read

The Business News. Companionship
Is what this being needs, and gets.
So now he shows his blue,
Climbs by his beak,

And chuckles, clicks, and snaps,
Because his friend and driver, with us
From Sunday lunching in the country
House, across the field at last comes back.

Going home, after years,
I was astounded to find
The great fir in which
Owls nested, dead.

I did recall the reeds
"Bending on the damp
Confines of the kingdoms
Of the air."

And children of children
I had known, laughed,
Laughed on the green
Garlick of white stars.

Evenings

Dawns being after all on tap
Wheresoever we are,
Admit to me when you last saw
The Morning Star?

Living inside our
Port-holed ark
We see with despondence
Every day go dark.

Obvious Disorder

This hot day in March, month
Of my birth, I do detest;
Living is, if not contradicted,
Not confirmed. There are no leaves
To reflect the sun unexpected,
Nothing yet is begun.
A grey scab covers the red wall border,
To-morrow it may be snow,
Yesterday it was wind also.
I look through trees, which do not,
As they will do happily,
Conceal disorder.

The Twice Striking Clock

I lie with both hands under my head
Not in the attitude of one who is dead.
A one-eyed dog, a fish, a prancing horse.
Dippings, chippings, of small flight traverse such sky
As shows between these white clouds and my eye.
This being the innocuous pause for everything,
No feared insects alight slyly and sting.
The clock on our hill strikes its second five,
Cramped, I creak up, so far not sad to be alive.

No Need of Crying

"As if to weep over one's own grave"—
But would it be so contemptible,
And so ridiculous, to weep over your own
Grave; if you had a grave,

And were not ash, a little in scattering
Caught in niches of a yew, most
Having sunk to the numberless
Root-hairs of our lawn?

You would weep over your own grave
Not for you, but because living had
One less who was conscious of living,
And light had one less who was conscious

Of light, and objects and *Gestalten*
Of objects; one less devotee;
Because after-dying, in short,
Is no break of renewable day

(But fortunately, no aching
Rheumatism also of the perpetuity
Of night or of nothing). O
If you could over your

Own grave cry, living you would be,
Light's admirer you would be, still
For the moment should I have
No need of crying.

Privacies

What with cold clear days this year
The leaves are late
And birds, it seems to me, fidget
Around and have to wait.
Treading and accepting tread are privacies.
I recognize a half-song, I see coloured
Primaries and breast
Of newcomers fidgeting through the bare neighbourhood
Of their last season's nest.
Privacies are treading and accepting tread,
So too rounding for the frailty of the eggs,
With the pushed breast the feathers of a bed.

While

I don't say what throat, or know—
I say only, sings
In the uncontaminated hollow of this

Morning, say only, sings.
I say not then, not there. Now, only,
Sings in the uncontaminated

Hollow of this morning. Sings, only,
Of the uncontaminated hollow
Of this morning, now, and sings.

Light Thoughts
of Marinetti and Balla

i

Let's Murder the Moonlight.
We did not have much light,
Marinetti, so you urged
In that writing
The murder of light.

Street Lamp, Study of Light:
Once worshipful
Luna in crescent, Balla,
In that picture, you
Hide with your light.

ii

Hold up your light,
Fill your mouth with the red,
In this cave create,
In this light of the night.

Snuff your small light,
Now in the beast's fur of darkness
Feel your way out: it is now
Stars of the night,

And (Sky Lamp, Study of Light)
Maybe a moon. Or
A comet of fibres of light
Streams in the night.

iii

You have murdered the moon and the night,
Switched on the light,

You have opened his eyes by force,
And poured in your light,

Marinetti, Balla,
Poured in your light.
Into his comfort of night have
Torturers poured in your light.

Picture in a Closed Book

I keep a picture in a shut book,
A coloured lithograph, bound in.
Each time I open this shut book I think
Why don't I cut this splendid picture out
And hang it up inside a frame?
And at once I shut this book again.

The Green Park

Wet. The deckchairs are still out.
Great leaves yellow the worn ground.
No holders of hands or assailed lone
Elderly walkers either are around.

It rains more. More watercolour leaves are
On the way down. Red lights, red
Danger in close ranks, even now perfect,
Are the late geraniums.

I could think, No, there are none happy
Or not happy and no biggest city around
Or one only in which for a reason unknown
There is no living; not a human sound.

Repetition, in a Yew Tree

Inside the gloom of the small leaves
A new nest.

On which platform the she-bird
Has laid. Two clear eggs push
Into the hot feathers of her breast:

Whiteness not to be seen inside this tree
Named ages ago a tree of Always
And a tree as well of Death.

Storm Coming in Wales

A cloud shoulders—it seems suddenly—up
Over this unsunned Welsh hill. It is the ovoid
Top which is to be seen most grandly and whitely. Full.

But I concern myself momently now more with the dense
Teasing blackness which is forming against this hill.
There is no sun, lightning must be soon. I try,

Try to see into this plum-toned great blackness, this
Opaqueness in dimensioned stillness. I smell the air. I see—
And you not here—pink as the pink soap you used some roses.

Nearly Extinct

Many warm creatures now
burn bright alone in worn-out phrases,
and their indifferent extinguishers
maintain themselves in cages.

Our new Edwardian interrupts his slumber
And stacks upon the flats of Humber
Photocopies of ridiculous lumber.

Ungrateful

"I'm not so often in the news,
They don't give me such long reviews,
I've licked the public arse
Since I was young
And now the arse prefers
Another tongue."

In Extremis

You know a Fleet Street trick or two,
You put death into all you do
And poets kill themselves for you.

First it was poor Mrs. Hughes
You kept a long while in the news,
Selling her ovened in reviews.

Now Berryman's walked off his bridge,
Extinguished by the cold, poor midge,
And that keeps up your average.

And two to one on who is next
Beyond the remote Bermudas vext,
Since *in extremis* is your text.

But if another of your crew
Must drown in existential stew,
It could, it might, it may be you,

And that believe me, I'd regret
Because I keep you for a pet,
And do not want to lose you yet.

As One Who Spoke Daffodils

As one who spoke daffodils
Not creating his perception of daffodils,
Not at all because flowers of daffodils
Were for example yellow or yellow-powdery,

Now this one
Speaks black
Without black,
Shriek
Without shriek,

Crow
With only the sentimental
Obscenity of
Crow.

First Public Death of the
New Year Season

Today we celebrate the death or rather
Mourn the concluded span of that
Little man
Whose say-so dropped the atom bombs;
By which began
As well the acts of Vietnam.

Of the two present Filths of Vietnam
One says "He was a giant of our times".
The other Filth of Vietnam
Says he led his nation with determination, so
Preparing his own grand
Strategies of filth in Vietnam.

At home our constitutional machine, our
Queen, cables we English always will
Remember this thin-lipped little man
And "his great personal and public qualities",
By which began
The bloody filth of Vietnam.

The Times, O god the Times, says a less uncomplex
Man could never have decided to release
Those bombs upon Japan.
And I reflect that the mentally
Uncomplex ichneumon
Equivalently rhymes with Truman.

I mean that sneaking fly which comfortably lives
By making others die; as inconspicuous as
That little man
Whose simple thinking ran that all
The life of man
Must either cease or be American.

On If You Are

Digging the world or
Fixing on a star,
Everything depends
On if you are.

Possibly orgasms
Happen in the head,
You think of Pompadour, the footboy's
In her bed.

And going the whole way
In the funeral car
Living is the moments
When you are.

Dreaming, or clasping
In the bed,
Aliveness is
Before you're dead.

So the trees go on, adding
To themselves a little each season,
It is true not talking,
Not walking around, at night.

Sensitive slowly, open
To being by shorter-lived
Men felled. Houses as well
Below them go on,

Sheltering intricate
Consciousness. And that is dissolved.
And the hall-door opens, and horizontally
Do emerge the dead,

The left rooms—even
The bedroom—being only indifferent.
Only on *Populus tremula*—aspens—do leaves
Shiver; which is the breeze.